My First Book about the Animal Alphabet of Tropical Rain Forests

Amazing Animal Books Children's Picture Books

By Molly Davidson

Mendon Cottage Books

I0439611

JD-Biz Publishing

Read More Amazing Animal Books

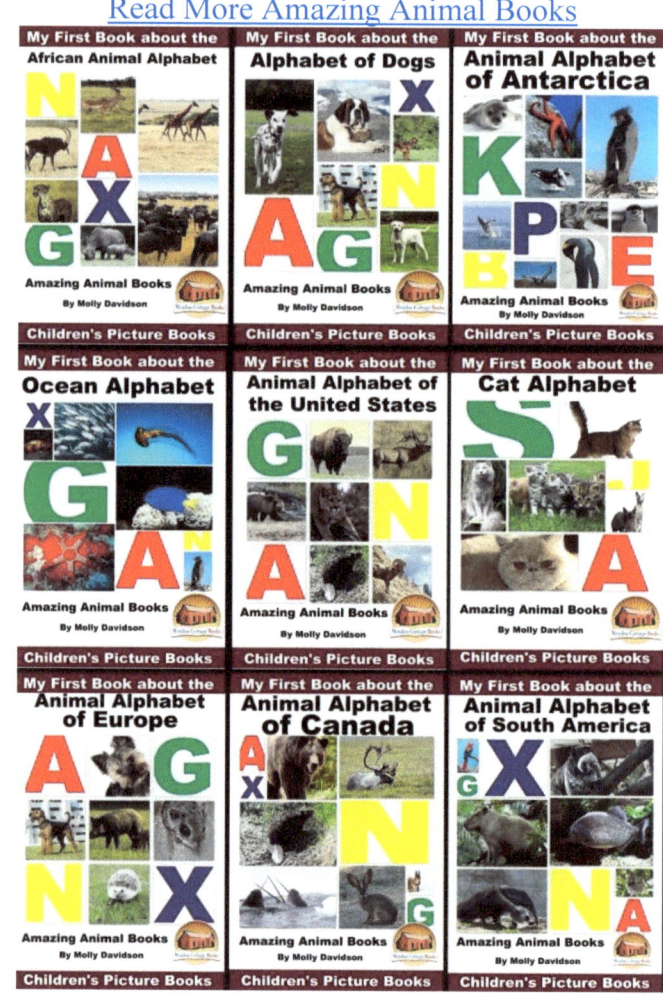

Purchase at Amazon.com

Download Free Books!
http://MendonCottageBooks.com

Introduction

Tropical rainforests are found near the equator and get more than 8 1/2 feet of rain per year!

More animals live in the rain forest than all other habitats combined.

 **is for an Anteater.**

Anteaters don't have a very good eye sight, but they have an amazing sense of smell.

They use their sharp claws to break into an ant's nest, in order to eat the ant inside.

 **is for a Baboon.**

![Baboon with a baby baboon sitting on the ground in front of green foliage.]

Baboons usually live in groups, called troops, of 35 - 50.

They eat grass, roots, fruit, and flowers.

C is for a Chameleon.

Chameleon usually change color to help control their body temperature or to talk to other chameleons.

To catch their food, they will sneak up very quietly then flick their tongue extra fast.

D is for a Death Adder.

Death Adders are some of the most venomous snakes in the World, and usually kill humans unless given antivenom.

The girls are larger than the boys.

They're related to cobras, mambas, and coral snakes.

E is for an Emerald Tree Boa.

Emerald tree boas live in the Amazon, and grow to be about 7.25 feet (2.2m) long.

They hunt small animals at night; they eat their prey head first, then rest for several weeks while digesting their kill, before eating again.

 **is for a Flying Frog.**

Flying frogs don't really fly, they jump and glide through the air using their webbed feet and flaps of skin.

They grow to be about 4 inches (10 cm) long.

G is for a Gorilla.

Gorillas will build their nests in the trees; this is where they sleep at night.

They beat on their chests to scare off intruders or threatening animals.

The male (boy) which is in charge of the group is called the silverback.

 **is for a Honeycreeper.**

Honeycreepers eat fruit, nectar, and some types of insects.

I is for an Iguana.

Iguanas are about 6 - 7 feet (2 m) long.

If they are in danger they break off their tail, don't worry they will grow a new one.

They like to live high up, about 40 - 50 feet (12 - 15 m) in the trees to avoid predators.

J is for a Jaguar.

In South America, the word "jaguar" means the hunter that kills with a single leap.

They have such sharp, strong teeth; they can bite through turtle shells.

They are related to panthers.

 is for a Keel Billed Toucan.

Keel billed toucans have large, brightly colored bills, that can be as long as 1/3 their body.

They are not very good at flying, do they usually just hop from tree to tree.

They eat fruit, insects, bird's eggs, and frogs.

L is for a Lemur.

Lemurs have forward pointing eyes and long tails which help them jump from tree to tree.

They are related to monkeys, but have a much better sense of smell than them.

They can only be found on the island of Madagascar.

M is for a Mouse Deer.

They are not a mouse or a deer; they have their own group called tragulidae.

Mouse deer weigh between 11 - 18 pounds (5 - 8 kg) and stand about 2 1/2 feet (73 cm) tall.

They have two long fangs which they use to fight each other with.

 **is also for a Macaw.** (* Bonus Letter)

Macaws have large beaks that they use to break apart nuts and seeds.

They live for about 60 years in the wild.

 **is for a Newt.**

Newts hunt for meat, mostly at night.

They have toxins that can ooze from their skin.

Newts can restore almost every body part, like their legs, arms, tail, eyes, and heart.

 **is for an Okapi.**

Okapi look like zebras, but they are related to giraffes.

Their blue tongue is so long they can use it to clean their eyelids and inside their ears.

They mark their territory with a tar like substance from their feet.

P is for a Python.

Pythons are about 16 feet long.

They wrap their long bodies around their prey and squeeze them until they die.

If they eat something large, they can go over a year without eating again.

 **is for a Quetzal.**

Quetzals have brightly colored tail feathers which can be up to 3 feet (1 m) long.

They eat fruit, worms, frogs, larvae, insects, and snails.

They are in danger of extinction.

R is for a Red Panda.

Red pandas are more closely related to raccoons than bears.

They can spend up to 13 hours per day looking for bamboo to eat; they also eat insects, eggs, and small animals.

S is for a Swallowtail Butterfly.

Swallowtail butterflies are the largest butterflies in the World.

There are over 550 species of the swallowtail butterfly; most of them live in the tropics.

T is for a Tarsier.

Tarsiers are only about 3 - 6 inches (8 - 15 cm) long, but with their long tails they measure almost 11 inches (28 cm).

Just one of their eyes is heavier than their brain.

 **is for an Umbrellabird.**

Francesco Veronesi © <u>Wikimedia Commons</u>

Umbrellabirds have a big puff of black feathers on top of their head, which looks like an umbrella.

V

is for a Viper.

Viper snakes are usually pretty short and have wide, plump bodies.

Vipers have two hollow fangs which can be tucked toward the roof of their mouth, until they are ready to be used to strike prey.

Venom is released through the fangs which helps kill their prey.

 **is for a Woolybear.**

The woolybear is a caterpillar that changes into a Isabella Tiger Moth.

They eat grass and wild flowers.

Woolybears are about 1 1/2 inches long.

 **is for a Xenops.**

Xenops birds live in the tropical forests of Mexico, Central and South America.

They find food by hitting open dead tree branches and eating the insects inside.

They lay 2 white, glossy eggs at a time, which take about 16 days to hatch

Y

is for a Yellow Jacket.

Yellow jackets are a type of wasp.

Only the girl yellow jackets can sting, and unlike a bee they can sting multiple times.

The boys and worker wasps will die over the winter, only the queen will survive.

Z is for a Zorro.

A Zorro is a small dog like fox that hunts at night in the rainforest of South America.

They're about 2.5 - 3 ft (72 - 100 cm) long; with a tail that is about 12 in. (30 cm) long, and weighing between 20 - 22 lbs (9 - 10 kg).

Conclusion

There are many animals that live in the tropical rainforests; we hope you have enjoyed learning about a few of them.

One final fact, rainforests stay between 93°F - 68°F (34°C - 20°C), all year long.

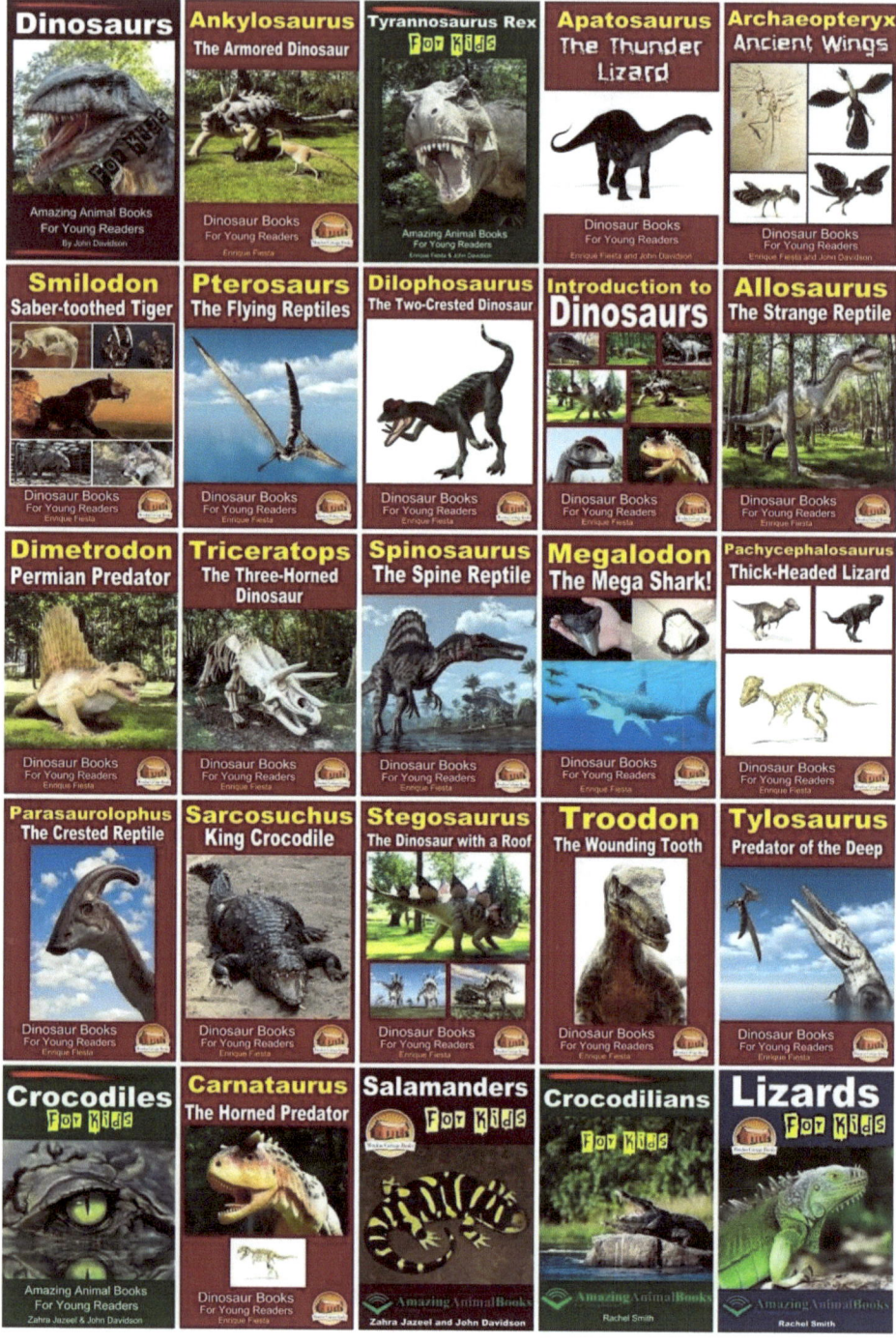

Our books are available at

1. Amazon.com

2. Barnes and Noble

3. Itunes

4. Kobo

5. Smashwords

6. Google Play Books

Download Free Books!
http://MendonCottageBooks.com

Publisher

JD-Biz Corp

P O Box 374

Mendon, Utah 84325

http://www.jd-biz.com/